THESE POEMS NEED HOMES
I MAKE STUFF UP

Dominic "Flominic" Farrenkopf

Cover image illustrated by Dominic "Flominic" Farrenkopf
Author Photo by Wayne Wardwell

authorHOUSE®

AuthorHouse™
1663 Liberty Drive
Bloomington, IN 47403
www.authorhouse.com
Phone: 1 (800) 839-8640

Published by AuthorHouse   03/14/2017

ISBN: 978-1-5246-7514-1 (sc)
ISBN: 978-1-5246-7513-4 (e)

Library of Congress Control Number: 2017903537

Print information available on the last page.

TABLE OF CONTENTS

Stories 1

Day Off...3

The Talisman 5

All Over The Place 8

The April Fool 10

The Pad 12

Rusty Treasure 14

My Easter Basket..16

Condor Four 18

Inhale..20

Nine Months..22

Dreamers...24

In Bloom 26

Side Effects...28

Hopes..30

Her Dad..32

Summertime 34

Some Body..36

Light It Up 38

Road Trip..40

Yields 42

Purple Gold..44

My Curse 47

Cleaning House 49

Tie One On 51

The Store 53

A Distinguishing Taste...55

Mopping Up 57

Green Blessings 59

The Halfback 61

Together Time 64

Warmer 66

Dexter...68

October...71

Steak...73

Old Tricks..76

Countryside Views...78

Going South...81

Table Talk..83

Going Back...85

Slowing Down..87

Ink..89

Homemade..91

Gifts..93

Scraps..95

Up Late..98

Slimmer..100

Strands...103

Expecting..106

The Fling...108

Torture...111

Daytime Doctor...113

Desire...115

Arrival..117

Morning Attire..119

BONUS POEMS

First Story...123

Breakfast...124

Pirate..125

Petals..127

Guess What...128

Dedication

For Cakes, who courageously endures…
all the stuff I make up.
and
For Peebs, the perfect travel companion-
who could walk backwards and eat wallboard at the same time.
I am not making this up.

PREFACE

Dominic Farrenkopf is a Bitterroot Valley treasure. Over the past five years, his poetry has delighted readers of the Ravalli Republic newspaper each weekend with their fanciful but poignant glimpses of everyday life. In this volume, he's compiled the poems published in his third year with the Republic. There are odes to the "recess ladies" and a temptress puppy, reminiscences of huckleberry picking and Christmas tree hunts, and somber tributes to the selfless sacrifices of our nation's heroes.

Flominic, as he's known to many, is generous to a fault. He shares his poems and love of verse with the residents of Sapphire Lutheran Homes, where he is activities director; with students in classrooms all across the valley; and with the fans who pack his occasional bookstore and civic group appearances. Each summer, he's at the Ravalli County Fair, organizing and enlivening the poetry competition. He writes verses for special events, at the request of friends and strangers alike. He donates his time and considerable creative talents and energy to myriad causes and community organizations, raising money and spirits day in and out.

I'm so proud to introduce this little volume of poetry. It's a warm and wonderful day when you can spend a few minutes in the company of leprechauns and naughty schoolchildren and a tiny baby born in a manger. I know you'll feel that grace and gentle spirit in these pages as well.

Sherry Devlin
March 6, 2017

Stories

On my way in to work
I scheme while I drive,
by telling wild stories
is how I thrive.

Today's was a gem
I couldn't wait to try.
I call it entertainment.
They say, I lie.

"Guess who's coming
to visit us all next week?
It's my twin brother.
The guy's really a freak."

"He works for the circus
as an acrobat.
His signature move
is falling on the mat."

"He deliberately misses
the safety net.
We're all surprised
That Frederick's not dead yet."

They all look at me
expecting a punch line.
I just walk off
giving no telltale sign.

So you see,
to fill my proverbial cup,
I just hang around all day…
and make stuff up.

March 8, 2014

Day Off

This morning at work
around the coffee pot,
whistling and blowing kisses,
was my friend, Scott.

"Good morning!" he shouted,
with a broad, wide grin.
I asked him about
the fine mood he was in.

"There's no doubt," he said,
"it's cloud nine that I'm on."
"Somethin' happen yesterday,
when you were gone?"

"Oh, yes, it did.
I had the most epic day!
I went for coffee
and didn't have to pay."

"I had a free one coming
on my punch card.
I sat and did the crossword-
the one that's hard."

"I strolled to the library
picked out a book,
then read for an hour
in a cozy nook."

"I walked back home
and got out my mountain bike.
I rode to the river
and took a shore hike."

"I pedaled home,
had lunch, and then took a nap.
I slept for hours
in my favorite wrap."

"I went out for dinner
and then caught a show,
wound down with a nightcap
sipping nice and slow."

"Seems like yesterday
really did do the trick!
How'd you get off work?"
"Simple...I called in sick!"

March 15, 2014

St. Patrick's Day always offers a wealth of inspiration for Irish folklore. I love writing poems about leprechauns but would never want to meet one.

The Talisman

I was down on my luck
and needed a change
so I went to see
Old Man Colin- "The Strange".

They called him "The Strange"
'cause of the stuff he did.
But what did I know?
I was still just a kid.

The old man's real name
was Colin O'Keefe,
and he was as Irish
as real corned beef.

He had a bright red beard,
he was stout and round,
and he stood only four feet
off of the ground.

He'd puff his pipe on the porch
and stroke his beard,
and sing old songs and chants
in a voice quite weird.

I went to Colin
with my hat in my hand,
and asked for secrets
of the ancient green land.

He grinned at me.
"So, it's luck you need, my lad?
You've come to the right place,
though most think I'm mad."

"My grades are poor
and I didn't make the team."
"I've got just what you need,"
said he with a gleam.

"For grades I could give you
a four-leafed clover.
Touch it each night–
school troubles are over."

"A lucky coin
carried in your left pocket,
you'll run on the field
fast as a rocket."

"A horseshoe, ladybug
or dried out wishbone
will bring great fortune
and you'll ne'er be alone."

"But for you, my boy
I've saved the best for last,
I'll share with you
a talisman from the past."

He leaned forward
and on his pipe, took a draw.
He held in his hand
a severed rabbit's paw!

Laughing he said,
"This foot will bring lots of luck.
Just look what it did
for the poor doe or buck!"

My hair stood on end
just like a church steeple,
O'Keefe was sure
one of the Little People!

My blood ran cold
I was shaking like a leaf.
He reached it to touch me-
I lurched from O'Keefe!

I turned tail and ran
my heart raced with fear.
He missed with the hare's foot...
that's why I'm still here!

March 22, 2014

All Over The Place

Two recess ladies
stood by the tire swing,
watching the children
and talking about spring.

"You know, Liz, I saw
my first robin last week,
and the ice is breaking up
along the creek."

"Yeah, Jen, my cat stays
outside a whole lot more,
and there's never ice
in her dish by the door."

"I'm glad I don't have
to scrape my windshield,
and the farmer next door
has plowed his field."

"My daffodils are peeking up
their small heads
in neat little bunches
through my flowerbeds."

Just then two brown squirrels
zipped up a tree trunk
two dancing finches
fell from a branch-ker plunk.

Sallie and Genny raced
Brian and Billy.
They squealed and laughed
all acting quite silly.

A group of small girls
was hunting down one boy.
His face didn't show fear
his smile spelled joy.

The monitors watched
as the little boy fled.
Jen looked over at Liz
and smiling, she said,

"You know that it's spring
when all over the place
all the boys and girls...
are busy playing chase!"

March 29, 2014

<u>The April Fool</u>

I love my mother dearly
and that's the honest truth,
but when April comes around,
she becomes "Ruthless Ruth".

The night before April first
she short-sheeted my bed,
and put dye in my toothpaste
which turned my teeth bright red.

She set my alarm to ring
at three in the morning.
At six o'clock she blew
an airhorn without warning.

My clothes were laid out for me
backwards and inside out.
There was newspaper in my shoes,
and they smelled like trout.

On my way down to breakfast
I stumbled in the hall.
She set up a trip wire
hoping that I would fall.

I turned on the kitchen tap
so my thirst could be quenched.
She put a twist tie on the sprayer
so I got drenched.

She put strings in my pancakes,
I couldn't cut them up,
and my apple juice was frozen
solid in my cup.

She packed a mayonnaise
and sawdust sandwich for my lunch,
and to go with it
a thermos of salty fruit punch.

She glued my hat to my head
and sent me to school.
Just try starting your car, Mom...
I'm nobody's fool!

April 5, 2014

<u>The Pad</u>

I stopped by my friend's
after work for a beer
I said, "Wow, Brad,
I like what you've done in here!"

"That deer head looks great
hanging over your couch,
next to the beaded, leather
tobacco pouch."

"That blue Camaro SS
poster's a beaut.
Same with the John Elway
mile-high salute."

"Brad, do you think this place
needs a woman's touch?"
"Not really. I don't see how
that would help much."

"For starters, I can
come and go as I please,
and don't have to cover
every cough or sneeze."

"And all of those sounds
that amuse little boys
are welcome in my house
and not termed rude noise."

"When I want a snack
I eat over the sink,
and straight from the carton
I can take a drink."

"Speaking of drinks,
I've always got one on tap.
I like to a have a cold one
after my nap."

"I eat what I want
any time, night or day,
and I can always watch
my favorite teams play."

"I don't fold clothes
they come straight from the dryer.
I crank loud music
in this--my empire."

"I don't know why
I'd mess this up with a wife.
There's really nothing like...
the bachelor's life!"

April 12, 2014

Every spring I write a garage sale poem and they are all drawn from actual experiences and a little exaggeration. This poem is no exception.

<u>**Rusty Treasure**</u>

This time of year
my husband's described with one word.
Well, actually it's two
and they are: "early bird".

Saturday mornings he's awake
before sunup
and he fills to the brim
his "to-go" coffee cup.

With newspaper in hand
he heads out to his truck,
and tears out of the driveway
hoping for good luck.

He always returns
just before it's time for lunch.
His pickup truck's filled with junk-
I mean a whole bunch!

He hops around
like a kid in a candy store,
talking wildly about
his treasures galore.

"I got these rubber decoys
all for just two bucks!"
He held up a squashed strand
of faded mallard ducks.

"Look at these old bottles
shaped like trucks, trains and cars!
They came in a box
with these blue medicine jars!"

"I bought license plates
and this electric heater!
All for five dollars-
I feel like a cheater!"

"Linda, I got you a carrier
for your cat!"
"Larry, how nice,
but you didn't have to do that."

"Look at this raft
I got for a ten-dollar bill!"
The boat was my breaking point,
now I'd had my fill!

"Week after week
you bring home more "rusty treasure",
and now our garage is
filled up beyond measure!"

"Larry, my love,
let's not let our marriage fail.
You get out there...
and have your own garage sale!"

April 19, 2014

<u>My Easter Basket</u>

On Easter morning
I woke up around dawn,
and rushed to find the eggs
hidden on the lawn.

The fun and excitement
I just can't mask it,
I laughed gleefully
and rushed to my basket.

The bunny left it
on the patio chair.
He must know I'm short
and I can reach it there.

I scamper through the grass
finding the treasures,
then rush in to see
how my basket measures.

Some eggs are hard-boiled,
others are plastic,
filled with trinkets and money—
how fantastic!

There's chocolate eggs
filled with caramel and cream,
and marshmallow chickies
that taste like a dream.

A milk chocolate rabbit
who's hollow inside,
and a little lamb nightlight
for my bedside.

Peanut butter candy
shaped like a carrot,
Spring Blossom perfume-
I can't wait to wear it!

Barrettes for my hair
and a tiny gold ring.
It's all perfect
except for one little thing.

The one thing Easter Bunny
can take right back
are all of these jelly beans...
that are pitch black!

April 26, 2014
I love kites and don't fly them nearly as much as I would like. So,
to fill my kite-flying void, I wrote a poem about it.

<u>Condor Four</u>

Fresh out of my box today
I'm a Condor Four,
the highest-flying kite
you can buy at the store!

From top to bottom
I'm easily four feet tall,
with a width of three feet
I can fly above all!

I'm a brilliant blue
like the sky in the springtime,
with my white, ten-foot tail
I can quickly climb!

My frame and crossbeams
are a strong, lightweight steel,
my line equals twelve-pound test
on a fish reel!

And on my spool
there's five hundred feet of line.
I can string it all the way out
and still be fine!

I'm made of a fabric
that withstands any breeze,
and designed to take flight
with just a simple sneeze!

The birds all envy me
and the clouds pay respect,
but even the best
are occasionally checked.

I was off to soar the skies
to fly high and free,
but ten feet off the ground...
I got stuck in a tree!

May 3, 2014

I read somewhere that aromas trigger memories better than any of our other senses. After reading this poem, you'll see I'm inclined to agree.

Inhale

First thing this morning
I opened my garden shed.
The scent of gas, oil and tools
filled my head.

I inhaled deeply
and backed out the mower.
I adjusted the depth
to cut a bit lower.

The acrid aroma
of the newly cut lawn
brought a freshness to the air
shortly after dawn.

I walked through the wet grass
covered with morning dew.
I had tomato starts
and thought I'd plant a few.

The rich, heavy essence
of the garden soil
made it a pleasure to dig-
this was no toil!

The tomatoes were in,
so I got out some paint.
As I stirred, it's perfume
pricked my nose- light and faint.

I painted my storm shutters
and my window trim,
then decided to burn
the ditch grass on a whim.

The smoke rose from the grass
as a pungent incense.
It drifted through the pasture
and slipped out the fence.

I coiled my hose
and leaned my rake on the sill.
I touched off a match
to light my barbecue grill.

The charcoal's fragrant flame
inspired me to say,
"Ah, there's nothing like...
the smell of a Saturday!"

May 10, 2014

<u>Nine Months</u>

She says, "Good morning, dear!"
with a big wide smile.
"Guess what we will have
in just a little while?"

He looks into his young wife's
bright, brown gleaming eyes.
"You're on the nest!?"
he exclaims with joyful surprise.

Now begins her long journey
starting with "the glow",
and other women can guess
though she doesn't "show".

But now in the morning time
she feels quite sick.
Saltines and hot green tea
will sometimes do the trick.

Now she's craving foods
that are both odd and bizarre,
and he makes late night trips
to the store in his car.

She grows out of her clothes,
they are all way too tight,
and nothing in "maternity"
seems to fit right.

Her mood goes back and forth
like a loose playground swing,
and out of sympathy
he, too, eats everything.

They ask the doctor
to please not tell the gender,
and now she walks
like she's on an all-night bender.

It's not just her walking,
it's lifting and bending.
It seems that her pregnancy
is never ending.

She can't sleep at night
or stay awake in the day.
"Oh, please, get this baby out!"
she begins to pray.

When her time finally comes
she hollers out in pain.
She yells, "It's all his fault!"
and makes herself quite plain.

Hours of her torture
transforms to blissful joy,
when the doctor announces.
"Congrats, it's a boy!"

Those nine long months
and her labor pains seem mild,
when the first-time mother...
holds her newborn child.

May 17, 2014

Dreamers

Two small boys
were throwing stones into a pond,
both dreaming out loud
into the great beyond.

"I'd be a first-round pick
major league pitcher,
with a mean curve ball
called the 'grueling glitcher'!"

The next boy threw a rock,
"I'd be quarterback,
with hundreds of touchdowns
and never a sack!"

Two young ladies
sat at the base of a tree,
plucking petals to find
who their beau would be.

"I am sure mine will be
tall, handsome and kind,
and cure all diseases
with his brilliant mind!"

"I hope mine's a hero,
both brave and daring,
a fireman racing
with sirens blaring!"

A husband and wife
looked through real estate books.
"Our house should have a sunroom
and reading nooks!"

"An office, a basement
and a garden place,
a huge porch
and lots of entertainment space!"

They all do this often,
every chance they get,
and it never gets old
on that you can bet.

Because nothing beats sitting
with a best friend
and playing a rousing game of...
"Let's Pretend"!

May 24, 2014
I write a Memorial Day poem each year. In this poem, I explore the contributions made by the fair and the brave.

In Bloom

Petunia was pretty
but she chopped her hair,
carried a musket
and wore what men would wear.

During the revolution
she did her part,
and fought for independence
with all her heart.

Iris was a nurse
who cared for the fallen,
between the wounded
like a bee to pollen.

It was the Civil War,
our country was torn,
of neutrality
was her uniform worn.

Lilac was beautiful,
a U.S.O. girl,
who boosted morale
with a dancefloor whirl.

Her First World War garb
was a blue print dress,
and despite her sore feet
she always said, "Yes".

Violet was a SPAR
protecting our vast coast.
"Semper Paratus-Always Ready!"
she'd boast.

As a World War II
Coast Guard reservist,
she maintained bases
and cutters she serviced.

Blossom-Vietnam
Buttercup-yesterday
both soldiers in uniform
thick in the fray.

As these flowers emerge
and bloom in the spring,
draw your thoughts to those
who helped our freedom ring.

Remember those
whose devotion never swerved,
the courageous and faithful...
women who served.

May 31, 2014

Side Effects

I have arthritis
in my elbows and knees.
My doctor told me
she could put me at ease.

She prescribed me some pills
I could take each day.
The pain left my joints
but my skin all turned gray.

She prescribed an ointment
to smear on my skin.
My color came back
but I got really thin.

She prescribed me a pill
that would make me eat.
I gained some weight
but got blisters on my feet.

I get a biweekly shot
to cure those sores,
but now I have acne
coming out my pores.

So that prompted
another visit this week.
She said, "This is one more thing
we need to tweak."

"I cured your arthritis!"
my doctor would brag.
She did-but it's cost me
an arm and a leg.

It's a lot more money
my doctor collects,
prescribing different meds...
for the side effects!

June 7, 2014

<u>Hopes</u>

On the day of her birth
Great-Grandpa was there.
Then with loop letters
he carved her name with care.

He carved the face
of the chest lined with cedar.
Placed in her bedroom
it was there to greet her.

So were her grandmothers
with a patchwork quilt.
It went in first,
folded neatly and hand-built.

With the quilt
were embroidered pillowcases
and one dozen
antique "boy and girl" vases.

When she turned five
in went Grandma's gold locket.
The sides were worn
from time in Grandpa's pocket.

For her tenth birthday
she received white dishes
and flatware from her aunts
with "wedding wishes".

For Sweet Sixteen
she received guest book and quill,
and two silver goblets-
accepted with thrill!

At eighteen, cloth napkins,
cake server and knife,
and kitchen utensils
to start married life.

For her bridal shower,
her mother's veil,
placed on top
like a shimmering white sail.

She opens the lid
the morning of "her day".
Looking at her mom
she's not sure what to say.

She puts her veil on
and knows she's been blessed
by her family her whole life...
through her hope chest.

June 14, 2014

<u>Her Dad</u>

It started in a café,
just us in a booth.
He was in his prime,
I was just departing youth.

He stared quite hard at me
when I asked for her hand.
He sipped his coffee and said,
"What do you have planned?"

I told him, "Forever with
your daughter I'll spend."
He said, "This is what she wants
so I guess I'll bend."

Not long after our wedding
I saw him downtown.
It was around lunch
so we wolfed some burgers down.

With lemon-sweet iced tea
we washed them down the hatch.
We decided to go
to that night's boxing match.

The next weekend he needed
something heavy moved.
He decided to call me up-
my wife approved.

We started taking fishing
and then hunting trips.
My wife kissed me "bye"
with a smile on her lips.

She doesn't mind my going
with him to the bar-
just to watch hockey.
She knows I won't go too far.

Now it's in the same café,
chatting over pie,
laughing at his jokes,
it's easy to love this guy.

Before I was married,
a perk I never saw
was getting another dad...
my father-in-law!

June 21, 2014

<u>Summertime</u>

There are many indications
this time of the year
that tell us that summertime
might actually be here.

You'll start hearing lawnmowers
noisily cutting grass.
You'll smell late evening barbecues,
both charcoal and gas.

The temperature rises,
some days it will get quite high.
The daylight stretches longer
and the nights just zip by.

You'll see the swelling rivers
slowly start to subside,
and weekend weddings
all featuring a blushing bride.

Children walking, running, biking
and playing about.
They're all over the place
now that the schools are out.

The stores all display
their patio and camping gear,
and have raffles to win
a cheap cooler for your beer.

You'll see tank tops and shorts
come out now without fail,
revealing bare, white skin
that's quite sickly and pale.

You'll see the co-ed softball teams
take to the field,
but you know summer's here...
when bugs splat your windshield!

June 28, 2014

This poem was inspired by "scenery" I encountered on a visit to the grocery store. Of course, the people in the poem are imaginary, but I did see things I still can't unsee.

<u>Some Body</u>

Around this time of year,
when the temperature warms,
scantily clad people
will walk around in swarms.

Many of those people
have a lot more to show,
with their extra-large frames
and their caboose in tow.

One large woman was wearing
a bright pink tube top.
Without support,
it was more than a fashion flop.

A big man wore a t-shirt
with a cut collar,
with slit sleeves and sides
his stomach looked no smaller.

Perhaps he thought himself
the star of Muscle Beach.
Based on his exposed gut,
his toes he couldn't reach.

A plump lady in short-shorts
and a cut-off top
was sporting some body art
on her muffin top.

What likely started out
as a dolphin tattoo
had now swelled to resemble
a bloated Shamu.

Then there's the heavy guy
with the mesh-netting shirt.
Often with back numbers,
more often with front dirt.

Flip-flops and baggy shorts,
plumber's crack-just a bit,
but the grossest thing is
the shirt's a stretch-to-fit.

And people aren't staring
because you're admired.
They're thinking, "Oh man...
more clothes should be required!"

July 5, 2014

<u>Light It Up</u>

I couldn't light the paper
in the wood stove,
nor the wax candles
in the front room alcove.

I couldn't light his pipe
when dad had a puff.
I could blow out the match
with a windy huff.

I couldn't light candles
on my birthday cake.
Mom thought I'd burn my fingers,
for goodness sake.

I couldn't light trash
out in the burn barrel.
My mom thought it put me
in some great peril.

But each year I'd rush
to the fireworks stand
for pyrotechnics,
both the legal and banned.

I'd fill to the brim
my front and back pockets
with smoke balls, cherry bombs
and bottle rockets.

I had firecrackers
and Whistling Pete's
and M-80's to terrorize
the town's streets.

Mom normally kept them
behind locked latches,
but July 4th...
I got to play with matches!

July 12, 2014

For inspiration for this poem, I merely recalled childhood vacations.
I highly doubt, though, that my experiences were singular. I'm sure
many families shared vacations just like this.

Road Trip

Each summer my family
hops into the car
and travels to some map dot-
it's often quite far.

We start in good spirits
laughing and having fun,
when the squabbling begins-
started by my son.

"Mom! He's touching me
and is over on my side!"
"No, Mom, she started it
by kicking me!" he lied.

We pull into a rest stop
for a bathroom break.
Back on the road, "I have to go!"
For goodness sake!

We have lunch in the car.
A good idea I think.
We'll save some time
but then my daughter spills her drink.

My husband sings loudly
about bottles of beer
when, "Mom, the baby just barfed
all over back here!"

The hottest part of the day
the car vapor locks.
I stay with the kids
while my husband, for help, walks.

We get the car fixed.
To make up time we're needing,
we get pulled over
and ticketed for speeding.

Arguing, pinching, crying,
a back seat riot.
My husband shouts,
"Now a contest to be quiet!"

We're not even halfway
to our destination,
and from my family...
I need a vacation!

July 19, 2014

Yields

I go out each morning,
it leans on the shed,
ready for work,
though the paint's a faded red.

It has two medium wheels
with spoke rims.
She fastened them to the deck
held tight by shims.

The wooden deck is broad,
a full three feet wide,
built four feet long
so that all her stuff could ride.

The handles are two-by-fours,
shaped on the ends,
gripped with her strong arms,
admired by her friends.

She had holes drilled
in the deck to hold tools,
and brackets to secure
her picking stools.

She had bucket slots
and hangers for hoses.
I wish I also had
her knack with roses.

We'd empty it
and stand it up on its end.
We'd rest in its shade
and in "girl talk" we'd spend.

She willed her gardens-
veritable fields-
now I harvest
its bountiful food yields.

Though my load may be heavy,
light is my heart,
when I work our land...
with my gram's garden cart!

July 26, 2014

As a child, I would go picking with my family and friends. From what I remember about the effort it takes to collect this mountain treasure, this poem is spot on. The reward, however, makes it all worthwhile.

Purple Gold

During the hottest days
of the fine month of July,
I drive up into the mountains
and I'll tell you why.

There's an elusive fruit
that grows on little bushes,
far away from city life
with its shoves and pushes.

I leave the pavement,
the road becomes dusty gravel,
full of potholes and washboard,
where very few travel.

I park in a pullout
and hike up the mountainside
in search of "purple gold".
I know where they like to hide.

With my milk jug bucket
fastened safely to my belt,
in the sun I start to pick,
then gradually I melt.

The summer rays beat down
and sunburn my back and neck.
The sweat seeps out my pores
but across the hill I trek.

My parched throat screams for water.
I stand and take a swill.
My foot slips on a downed branch
and my bucket I spill.

I scramble to collect
the small round treasures I've lost.
I scurry to retrieve them-
they come at such high cost.

I pick through the evening
and endure the horsefly bite.
I only head back down
when I'm overcome by night.

I creep down the dirt road
slowly around each switchback,
hungry, sweaty, exhausted,
driving in the pitch black.

I have the windows down
and breathe in fresh mountain air.
Next day I display my haul.
My friends all gawk and stare.

"James, we know it's hard work,
but tell us your secret spot."
"I'll gladly share my plunder
but tell you-I cannot."

"We'll gladly accept fresh pie
or a creamy milkshake,
but how much torture
do you think your body can take?"

"My hands are stained
and have the occasional sticker,
but I love my life...
as a huckleberry picker!"

August 2, 2014

My Curse

My husband's loud snoring
had gotten much worse.
In seeking him help,
I acquired a curse.

They gave him a sleep study,
a routine test.
T'was my last night
of rejuvenating rest.

He came home with
a black humidifier
and a diagnosis
that was quite dire.

"You have sleep apnea,"
the doctor declared.
And for what came next
I was just not prepared.

He had a face mask
and fifteen feet of hose,
the mask strapped tight,
covering his mouth and nose.

The hose went from mask
to a little machine.
He looked like a space invader-
just not green.

A humming sound started
when he flipped the switch,
with a frequent sputter-
did it have a glitch?

He rolled on his side,
the hose scraped the night stand.
The noise made my skin crawl
like an icy hand.

Lying on his side
the mask began to leak,
and emitted a high-pitched,
whistling squeak.

I doze in and out
of dreamless sleep at night.
By 3:30, the mask
is no longer tight.

And it is that flopping
and fluttering sound
that keeps my head
in my pillow, tightly bound.

Until he wakes up
the gasket will just flap.
My curse is my nights...
with my husband's CPAP!

August 9, 2014

<u>Cleaning House</u>

The following true tale
is hard to explain.
I write as it happened
between Mary and Jane.

'Twas Saturday morning,
Mary came to the door.
Jane welcomed her in,
"Mary, don't slip on the floor."

The kitchen floor shimmered
just like a frozen lake.
"Jane, I've just had one cup
and I've brought coffee cake."

"There's coffee in the pot
and I'll get you a plate.
I can't sit down, Mary.
My house is such a state!"

So Mary sat down
and watched Jane in a panic.
"I've got to keep mopping!"
she exclaimed, quite manic.

Jane finished mopping,
then grabbed her feather duster.
She started dusting the house
while in a fluster.

Then Jane hit the bathroom
with a cleaning bottle.
She was wiping it all down
going full throttle.

She then did the windows
and got out her vacuum,
and quickly began running it
in her front room.

Mary broke her silence,
"Jane, can't you take a rest
and spend a little time, with me,
your lonely guest?"

"You're tidying up your house
like a hurricane!
I've never seen you this way.
Can you please explain?"

"I can't talk!" Jane yelled,
over the vacuum humming.
"Any minute now...
my cleaning lady's coming!"

August 16, 2014

<u>Tie One On</u>

The surgeon was operating
until the dawn.
He drives the backroads to the lake
to tie one on.

The grocer lifted boxes all day
like a pawn.
Exhausted, he slips to the stream
to tie one on.

The scientist squints down
as his specimens spawn.
Bleary-eyed he goes to the creek
to tie one on.

The construction worker
drops his bags on the lawn.
He just heads to the reservoir
to tie one on.

The dentist pulls teeth all day
and feels withdrawn.
He escapes down to the river
to tie one on.

The grease-covered mechanic
lies to use the "John".
Instead he hides under the bridge
to tie one on.

The veterinarian struggles
to save a fawn.
It lives, but he stays at the pond
to tie one on.

The rancher bucks bales
in the sun with his brawn.
All sunburned, he walks to the ditch
to tie one on.

Inside, they've hung signs that say:
"Fishing I have gone,"
grabbed their fly rods and left...
to go and tie one on!

August 23, 2014

The Store

I was tending to my yard
last Saturday morning,
when Mrs. Pickering stopped over-
without warning.

She was my new next-door neighbor.
She'd just moved to town.
She needed a favor
and I couldn't let her down.

"Could you mind
my little boy, Tommy, for just a bit?
I'm sure you can.
It's a simple task to babysit!"

Before I could reply,
little Tommy grabbed my hand.
Mrs. Pickering turned away
saying, "Oh, how grand!"

"If I'm watching you
I can't mow the grass anymore.
Hop into the car, Tommy,
we're going to the store."

I parked the car in the lot,
got out and grabbed a cart.
"I want the fire truck one!"
Tommy said with a start.

So we got the fire truck
and went inside to shop.
From the first moment to the last,
that kid wouldn't stop!

"Can you buy me some chips?
Can I have a cheap fruit pie?
I'm sure Mommy wouldn't mind
if I gave them a try."

"Can I have watermelon?
Will you buy me root beer?
How about king crab?
I haven't had that in a year!"

"Ooh! Frootie-Flips cereal
and German chocolate cake!"
He wanted candy, gum, toys-
I couldn't get a break!

I did buy him a doughnut
so I wouldn't seem mean,
but he still begged a quarter
for the sticker machine.

As I stacked the groceries
into the car's back seat,
I thought, "This took hours
to complete a simple feat!"

"It seems grocery shopping
was such an easy chore,
until I had to take...
a little kid to the store!"

<u>A Distinguishing Taste</u>

Each year I donate
my time and my palate,
and nibble food entries
equipped with ballot.

There are foods I garnish
with a blue ribbon,
and they're a pleasure to munch-
I'm not fibbin'!

There are entries, however,
that make me gag,
so I bring water
and a tongue-wiping rag.

I've had bread
that tasted like moldy cardboard,
and Bundt cake that couldn't
be cut with a sword.

Jam that tasted like
flavored wallpaper glue,
and ginger snaps tasting like
an old gym shoe.

Grandma's pickle recipe
passed through the years,
with turpentine dill brine
that brings me to tears.

On a cobbler I write
a note that teaches,
"Dear Home Baker,
that was a waste of peaches."

Salsa that burns,
cake that's dry as desert sand,
pie with burnt crust
and scones, both chalky and bland.

Then those entries
labeled "Experimentals",
gooseberry, rhubarb tarts
with spiced red lentils.

I have no choice
but to consume with my mouth,
with fears of ending up
six feet deep down south.

Sometimes I'd rather eat
gross, mucky pond sludge,
than the stuff I taste...
as a county fair judge!

September 6, 2014

<u>Mopping Up</u>

As a school janitor
I do more than mop.
In fact, my extra duties
just don't seem to stop.

I've scraped at least
three pounds of gum off the bleachers,
and covered up graffiti
about our teachers.

In the girls bathroom
a door broke loose from the stall.
They won't even hold the weight
of a girl that's small.

Speaking of broken,
there's the library bookshelf.
The boys shook their heads,
but it didn't break itself.

Today's school lunch of meatloaf
made three kids sick,
and that stuff stains carpet
if you don't clean it quick.

Forgotten combinations
and jammed-up lockers,
breaking up groups of
music-blaring punk rockers.

Scuffs on the gym floor,
a broken faucet handle,
skateboarders smoothing curbs
with wax from a candle.

There's been about fifteen toilets
we've had to plunge.
We've cleaned gym towels
some jock used as a bath sponge.

For us custodians
this year's looking quite bleak,
especially since school's been back...
just one week!

September 13, 2014

The phenomenon explored in this poem is common in rural Montana, but I don't think it is an isolated incident. I'm sure this happens…wherever gardens grow.

Green Blessings

This time of year,
as summer begins to fade,
"green blessings" come from those
who work with the spade.

In springtime they prepare
and till their soil,
then plant, water and weed
with endless toil.

And even if their garden's
a complete wash,
they always have a bumper
of summer squash.

In particular,
one long, skinny and green,
each gardener brings forth
hundreds to the scene.

They're compelled to share
their plentiful bounty
from town to town
and all over the county.

They fill paper bags
and boxes to the brim,
then "bless" kin and stranger
alike on a whim.

People accept them
with an awkward smile,
then go home and toss them
in the round file.

We've all heard of "blessings"
left in unlocked cars,
left on stoop and porch,
welcomed like acne scars.

Given with recipes
like, "Seasoned and fried,
bread, muffins,
and even pancakes can be tried!"

And just like clockwork
this happens every year,
but permit me to express
both loud and clear:

"It doesn't even matter
if it's teeny.
Don't bother 'blessing' me...
with your zucchini!"

September 20, 2014

The Halfback

It's Friday night lights.
I dress to take the field.
Fearless in my armor suit,
I will not yield.

My footwear is leather.
I lace them tight and quick.
I must avoid a misstep
if the grass is slick.

My tube socks are midcalf
and meet my pant-leg cuffs.
My pants are bright white
with no grass stains or dirt scuffs.

My red top fits snug
with its built-in shoulder pads,
giving a broad appearance
to us pint-sized lads.

And lastly on my head
comes my crown of glory.
As I clip my chin strap
I concoct this story:

It's fourth quarter, fourth and long,
and we have the ball.
Coach signals to me
and sends me in with the call.

We need a touchdown to win,
the call's a trick play.
I line up behind the fullback,
he'll lead the way.

The ball is snapped from center,
the handoff is swift.
The fullback goes right,
causing the field to shift.

He turns and pitches to me,
it's a flea flicker!
I roll left, breaking tackles,
because I'm quicker.

I look downfield
I have a man open wide.
I heave a perfect spiral
without breaking stride.

The receiver's hands are sure
like a sticky glue.
My pass is right on target,
flying straight and true.

He hauls it in for six points,
the crowd starts to shout.
My buddy shakes my shoulder
and I snap right out.

"The crowd is cheering
and we're leading out the team."
Reality returns
and I wake from my dream.

This uniform I described
is not football gear.
Mom says I'm too small
to play on the team this year.

I want to play halfback,
Mom fears a broken bone.
So, with the band, I march...
and play the saxophone!

September 27, 2014

<u>Together Time</u>

When you're visiting with
a really good friend,
you never want your
"together time" to end.

There are some tricks of the trade
you can deploy,
like setting up a "false time"
wall clock decoy.

You just set the hands back
an hour or two,
and then act surprised like-
"Well, I never knew!"

Another trick is:
"I just made a fresh pot."
And everyone knows
the adage of "waste not".

"As long as we're not
wasting this coffee drink,
we'd better finish these cookies,
don't you think?"

Husbands sometimes
want your visits to end quick,
so you can always employ
this little trick:

"Your supper's in the crockpot.
I'll be home soon."
It takes them a bit
to tire of this tune.

Making false appointments
can buy you more time.
You'd stay on even if
it cost your last dime.

These methods are proven
and all work just fine,
but I suggest you try
a favorite of mine:

Lie. Say you'll help your cousin
who broke her hip.
Then get with a great friend...
and take a road trip!

October 4, 2014
Don't try this at home.

Warmer

Now that the mornings
are starting much colder,
I feel it in my feet
and each shoulder.

My back is also cold
and my nose and ears,
but I've picked up
a few tricks over the years.

It's necessary
to get up out of bed,
and to outsmart the cold-
I just use my head.

I microwave my socks-
one minute each side.
My towel warms-
in the oven opened wide.

I wrap my robe
in an electric blanket.
Before bedtime
I take the switch and crank it.

I lean my slippers
against the baseboard heat.
Putting them on each morning
is a nice treat!

A heater's on a timer
by the shower.
It's on before my alarm,
by one hour.

I soak all my kindling
in kerosene.
It lights the first try,
if you know what I mean.

And once I put
all of these tricks together,
I can stave off all amounts
of cold weather.

And my outfit turns
all night in the dryer.
I could be warmer...
but I'd be on fire!

October 11, 2014

<u>Dexter</u>

My sister spotted him first
in the parking lot.
We sat down to figure out
how he could be caught.

"I think he's living underneath
that old white fridge.
I say we set out some milk,
but only a smidge."

"I agree, and think we should add
some tuna fish.
I'll run in and grab a bowl
and a little dish."

We set out the food-bait
near the junk and trash cans,
then hid beside some cars
to further lay our plans.

"We'll just bait him out
a little further each day.
We'll gain his trust first
and then he'll come out to play."

My sis was smart and said,
"There's inside stuff to do.
We need a litter box,
food and water dish, too."

"He'll also need a bed,
toys and a scratching post.
A trip to the vet–
but you know what he needs most?"

"He needs a name,
but we will get to know him first.
Now hurry! Let's go!"
We both rushed off with a burst.

We used up all of our savings
and bought the stuff.
But Sis knew that having it
still wasn't enough.

Along with the bait
we set for the orange kitten,
my sister set Mom up
with a note she'd written.

We made friends with the kitty,
sis released the note.
Inside a beautiful card,
this is what she wrote:

"Roses are red
please take the night off, dear Mother.
Dinner will be prepared by
me and my brother."

"Get comfy on the couch,
watch your favorite show.
There's something quite exciting
we'd like you to know."

"We've found our family
the perfect addition.
It's the kitty cat
of which we've all been wishin'!"

Mom read the note
and saw the dinner had been made.
Sis handed her the soft kitten.
That was well played.

He purred. We knew right away
we hadn't vexed her.
"What do you kids call him?"
"We like the name Dexter."

"I can tell you both
don't want this kitten to go.
So we must all make sure...
the landlord doesn't know!"

October 18, 2014

October

This morning I stepped outside
and breathed deeply in.
The air smelled cold
and was sharp against my bare skin.

I zipped my jacket up
and started off to work.
I rounded the bend-
my nose went up with a perk.

I smelled cut grass,
the last mowing of the season.
Mingled with burnt leaves.
Yard clean-up, stood to reason.

Further up the roadway,
another whiff of smoke.
A wood stove blew forth
a white aromatic cloak.

After work today
I walked to the football game.
The aroma of popped corn
from concessions came.

Its buttery bouquet
pooled the whole field,
mingled with loud voices
yelling, "Do not yield!"

At halftime I bought
a cup of hot spiced cider.
Its tang tickled my nose
like a feathered spider.

As I drank in its warmth,
I stared at the night sky.
It smelled like snow,
or at least a determined try.

My gaze stopped in the branches
of the shedding trees.
Their essence of sap and leaves
infused the night breeze.

Those cottonwood giants
stood watchful and sober,
as they too breathed deeply...
the scents of October.

October 25, 2014

<u>Steak</u>

I remember well
opening day as a lad.
We spent weeks preparing for it-
me and my dad.

My dad mastered scents
and honed his bugling skills.
His calls sounded so real
they gave me the chills.

We broke out our hunting gear
and went through the stuff.
Dad bought top-shelf gear
'cause, "Smart is better than tough."

If it was broken
it would have to be replaced.
While at the store
he bought some seasoning to taste.

"This spicy rub will go great
on our fresh elk steak,
harvested from the huge
Boone and Crockett we'll take!"

"I promise you steak, Son,"
he gave my back a slap.
"There's nothing like
freshly charbroiled elk backstrap."

We bought ammo
and sighted in our rifle scopes.
We left at four a.m.
with high spirits and hopes.

Dad scouted an area
that promised big bulls.
There were rocks to trip over
and for dad's feet, holes.

Through the darkness dad tripped
and dropped his rifle twice.
I whispered, "Don't swear, Dad.
Just think of the new spice."

Dad had spice on his mind
and didn't see the creek.
He fell in. I whispered,
"Weren't you here just last week?"

We headed up
a heavily wooded hillside.
Dad tripped on a branch
and cut his arm open wide.

We nestled into a spot
to wait for sunrise.
As daylight crept in
Dad and I got a surprise.

Other hunters were calling elk
and firing shots.
The mountainsides were crawling
with little orange dots.

We hunched beneath a tree
'til it started to snow.
Dad was cold, wet and bloody.
He said, "Well, let's go."

We trudged through the forest
and got back to the truck.
Dad said, shivering,
"Next time we'll have better luck."

"Give me some hand warmers
from the glove compartment,
and let's go buy some steak...
in the meat department!"

November 1, 2014

Old Tricks

After eighty Easters
one thing I know well
is come October
those "sale" eggs sure smell.

And in those years I've learned
eggs will peel paint.
So I smear the roads-
their stench can make you faint.

Toilet-papering homes
doesn't cause much harm.
Now I'm not steady
nor do I have the arm.

No more T.P.,
but I do soap windowpanes.
That takes less brawn
and more sneakiness and brains.

As a lad I had
outhouses to knock down.
Now it's trash cans
I topple over in town.

Saving firecrackers
from the Fourth is fun.
Now it's a bit harder
from the scene to run.

I pulled off these pranks
long after my bedtime,
and tonight I'm still up
after the eighth chime.

That's when older
trick-or-treaters start to show.
I was set to "trick" them all,
row after row.

I sat in my lawn chair
with my garden hose,
to soak those goblins
from their heads to their toes.

My wife took the sprayer
and turned off the spout,
giving away my position
with a shout.

"Russell! Grow up!
You're eighty-two, not sixteen!"
Normally she's right...
except on Halloween!

November 8, 2014

Montana's Bitterroot Valley boasts beautiful countryside views that are marred by campaign signs before each election. Before writing this poem, I consulted with others and I found I'm not the only one annoyed by those signs.

<u>Countryside Views</u>

I was on the highway
watching for my turn.
I missed my exit
which caused for great concern.

The road was clearly marked,
that wasn't the prob.
My view was blocked
by those vying for a job.

A plywood sheet screamed,
"Elect me this season!"
Their name was written,
but there was no reason.

It was surrounded by
smaller boards of wood,
proclaiming that a new
"leader" would be good.

There were many others
black, blue, red and green,
blocking the road sign
so it couldn't be seen.

I flipped around
and turned on the country lane.
The litter on the roadside
boggled my brain!

Posters were nailed
to every tree and post,
touting the candidates
that would help the most.

I watched for my access,
I was out fishin'.
It was behind a
"panel politician".

I spent the afternoon
along the river.
Driving towards home
the sunset made me shiver.

I stopped to photograph
the majestic view,
blemished by a billboard:
"Our party will do!"

Driving home I decided
to count them all.
Well, I failed,
and not 'cause my brain is small!

There are hundreds of them
everywhere you look.
I'm so glad that now,
the vote is in the book.

So, officials, work
and cross those party lines.
But before you do that...
go take down your signs!

November 15, 2014

Going South

When the frost sets in
and the leaves start to fall,
migrant birds emit
their "traveling south" call.

One species' nests
have been empty for some time.
With fledglings all grown,
they're in their adult prime.

The temperature drops
they start honking out loud.
Beeping their RV horns-
the highways they crowd.

Fifth-wheels join the flocks
all heading southbound,
driven by seniors
with silver hair they're crowned.

Highly active seniors
crowned like the royals,
loving the southern climate
and its spoils.

They winter in groups
having fun every chance.
A pack playing golf
or spinning a square dance.

Men strut about
shooting pool without guilt.
Women preen and twitter
while sewing a quilt.

Men gaggle daily
for rounds of pickleball,
while coveys of women
flock the Bingo hall.

Colonies of pairs
swoop in for flea market,
mustering RV's
and a place to park it.

This annual descent,
a sight to behold,
like double pinochle
in a hand you hold.

Make way for these nomads
traveling in herds,
seen across our land...
American Snowbirds!

November 22, 2014

Table Talk

Each Thanksgiving
my family comes from far and near,
and as we eat dinner
many stories I'll hear.

This year will be different.
No matter how I try,
I won't hear of the stocks
my brother "got to buy".

Instead I will listen,
and I'll be glad to learn,
'bout the allowance
my brother's kid "got to earn".

I'm sure my cousin
will talk about her boyfriend,
and how he likes to take her
to the mall and spend.

I won't hear that,
but her little sister will tell
how she brings the stuff home
to post online to sell.

My uncle wants to argue
about politics.
His little girl wants to show us
her new card tricks.

My sister will brag
about the bonus she got.
Her son will tell
it was a fruit basket with rot.

Grandpa will tell crass jokes
that make Grandma upset.
We'll tell 'knock-knock' jokes
and laugh 'til our eyes are wet.

No talk of government,
economy or banks.
No talk of weather or war-
for that I give thanks.

I'm likely to hear
a rhyming, limerick fable.
Because this year I'm sitting...
at the kids table!

<u>Going Back</u>

She's gone off to college
and lives across the state.
She quickly boards the bus
because she just can't wait.

This is her first trip back,
Mom and Dad are so proud.
"Let's go! Find your seats!"
she'd like to say to the crowd.

It took both of them
to pack the car yesterday.
With three kids they need lots
for a "week with Gram" stay.

They've decided to go
to his mom's place this year.
His dad passed this spring.
He fights back a brimming tear.

He boards the plane
dressed in civilian attire.
His "blues" sound alarms-
he's a distinguished flier.

Twelve out of eighteen
Thanksgivings served over seas.
He's going back this year
because his dad said, "Please?"

Her parents both greet her
down at the bus station.
They all embrace
and start trading information.

Five hours of driving
sure feels like dozens.
When they arrive
their kids race off with their cousins.

The plane landed.
He met his dad at baggage claim.
They laugh at his boot camp duffel
marked with last name.

They all gather around
a Thanksgiving dinner,
recycling jokes
about not getting thinner.

They clean up the dishes,
then serve coffee and pies,
play board games with laughter
and more jokes about size.

The evening winds down,
they all make their way to bed.
Travel and a full belly
make a sleepy head.

Before they close their eyes,
they look to heaven's dome,
and breathe a thankful prayer...
for this place they call home.

November 29, 2014

<u>Slowing Down</u>

Last year we ate
turkey dinner really quick,
then grabbed the paper
it was three inches thick!

We rifled through the ads
like a hurricane,
then drove into town
like a runaway train!

'Twas "Getting Dark Thursday",
we smashed our first door,
and trampled the manager
flat to the floor.

We shopped and shopped
until two in the morning,
then went to bed
'til the alarm clock's warning.

It was four a.m.
We joined the camped-out crowd.
We pounded the doors
and raised our voices loud.

We pillaged the stores
and we plundered them hard.
Soon I was maxed out–
so was my credit card.

I got home exhausted
and crashed on the bed.
Christmas last year
was no better, so instead...

We'll eat calmly,
then enjoy some pumpkin pie.
As for the paper,
we'll let the ads go by.

We'll enjoy the evening
and play some board games,
organize a gift exchange
by drawing names.

On Friday we'll sleep in
and not be nervous.
We'll miss all the crowds
and get better service.

We'll visit the shops
with storefronts small and quaint,
buying gifts there
makes you feel like a saint.

This year we're staying out
of the Black Friday race
and shopping for Christmas...
at a Mom and Pop pace!

December 6, 2014

__Ink__

Teacher made me go there
after shooting spitballs.
I used colored paper
and stuck them to the walls.

I got a great idea
while I was standing there.
If I could pull it off,
Teacher would have blue hair.

Making pens explode
would not be an easy task.
I could ponder it, though,
'cause I scared with a mask.

I wore a gruesome mask
and frightened my sister.
Dad said, "You stand there
and think about it, Mister!"

About my sister
I didn't have time to think.
Instead I imagined
a splashing of blue ink.

Things were just fine
until Mom caught me in the drawer.
I tried covering up
why I had pens galore.

"Benjamin!" she scolded.
"Put your nose in your place!
And drum up some remorse,
it just may help your case."

I'm sure not lamenting
or being a mourner.
I'm busy plotting my ink scheme...
in the corner!

December 13, 2014

<u>Homemade</u>

Two weeks before Christmas
we'd head to the woods,
dressed in boots, snow pants,
coats, mittens, hats and hoods.

We'd bring sled and saw
to cut our Christmas tree.
It seemed quite magical
that it would be free.

We'd find one, cut it,
then back to home we'd go,
tree on the sled,
us laughing and throwing snow.

We'd get it home,
it was usually too tall,
set in a bucket,
then wired to the wall.

With extra branches
we'd fill in the bare spots.
We'd drill the trunk,
then force branches in the slots.

Next we'd string up strands
of mismatched colored lights.
Mom used a ladder and broom
to reach the heights.

If half the lights weren't lit,
we'd shake the wire.
It was, "I changed that bulb.
Go ahead, try her."

Our ornaments were handmade
from years gone past.
Mom packed them safely each year
so they would last.

Made with playdough or wood,
covered with glitter.
"Look at this one you made!"
we'd laugh and twitter.

We'd hang the ornaments
and would only stop
when Grandma's corn husk angel
was placed on top.

As I think back fondly,
I smile with glee,
knowing we'd spent nothing...
on our homemade tree!

December 20, 2014

Gifts

We were all hanging out
by the bulletin board,
signing up for the party
like a starving horde.

Next to the entree selection
we wrote our name,
and then put a check mark
for the gift-exchange game.

Janet, a newcomer,
asked us all how to play.
We scrambled to explain
like kids on Christmas Day.

"You find a nice gift," said Sue,
"for ten bucks or so.
I shop the clearance rack
for stuff that has to go."

"That way it looks like
I spent more than the limit.
It only works
if you take the tag and trim it."

"No," said William, "don't try to buy
something that's nice.
Find something cheesy
that also has a low price."

"Wrap it up fancy
and give it a good disguise.
They open to get
a disappointing surprise."

Linda chimed in next
and said, "Listen here, Honey,
you can still play
without spending any money."

"Just find something at home
that is still in the box,
or an unlit candle
or a pair of new socks."

I said, "I'm fond of the style
of re-gifting.
I use gifts from years past
and just keep them shifting."

"I've got no shopping hassle
and spend nothing flat,
while making people think,
'Hey! I gave one like that!'"

"So, Janet, it may not be
very elegant,
but that's the way most of us play...
White Elephant!"

<u>**Scraps**</u>

Once, not so long ago
in a far distant land
lived a peasant man
with a crippled arm and hand.

The peasant man wandered around
from place to place
searching for odd jobs
then leaving without a trace.

One day a farmer heard
and answered the man's call
and gave him a week's work
cleaning out his stock stall.

The peasant accepted
and began right away.
At night he slept there
after cleaning it by day.

This same farmer
offered to a man and his wife
refuge in the shelter–
an answer to their strife.

She was expecting–
there was no room at the inn.
The farmer gave fleece scraps
to wrap her baby in.

The kind farmer
failed to mention the peasant.
Their coming startled him
in a way unpleasant.

But after more formal
introductions were made,
the topic turned to
where the child would be laid.

In cleaning the stall
the peasant man found wood scraps,
and fastened a manger
held tight with leather straps.

That same night the baby came,
just like He was due.
Then they wrapped Him up
in the fleece, quite soft but few.

The crippled man held the babe
and said not a word,
when a most fascinating
miracle occurred.

His tense arm relaxed
and his fingers unfurled.
He flexed smiling,
as if he'd received the world.

The man's crippled hand healed,
though twisted from birth.
Like the babe restored the arm,
He'll restore the earth.

He meagerly began
on scraps of wood and fleece,
come down from above to renew...
The Prince of Peace.

December 27, 2014

<u>Up Late</u>

'Twas the night before Christmas
and over at my house
I was putting together toys
purchased by my spouse.

I got my tool box out
and my electric drill.
I approached this task
full of confidence in my skill.

The first box I opened up
was a three-wheeled bike.
I thought, "This could be set up
by my own little tyke."

I dumped all of the parts
on the floor in a pile.
My wife just shook her head
at my haphazard style.

She asked, "Aren't you going to read
the instruction book?"
I scoffed at the pamphlet,
then tossed it without a look.

After an hour
I was singing a different tune.
"Dear, I may have tossed those out
just a little too soon."

"Well, you'd better hurry.
The kids are up before dawn,
and that's just the first of ten
I need you to work on."

I picked up the pace
and the little instruction guide.
I finally got it
by using the tool supplied.

Next up was a two-piece
plastic excavating set.
Snapping the pieces in half
was my one constant fret.

There was a dollhouse,
a wagon and a canvas kite,
four scooters and a beanbag game-
I'd be up all night!

The screws all looked the same
and the holes wouldn't align.
My fatigue just compounded
the toy's awkward design.

My wife brought out a plate
of cookies the kids had made.
"Please make sure you eat these."
Then 'goodnight' to me she bade.

This Santa wants to go to bed,
he's just so tired
but all these gifts say...
"Adult assembly required!"

January 3, 2015
Fad diets are very common, but they're at their strongest around the new year. This poem pokes fun at one of those diets.

<u>Slimmer</u>

I was at a New Year's party
having a snack,
when a guest sneaked up
and attacked me from the back.

"It sure looks like you're enjoying
that cookie tray!
It may not be my place,
but how much do you weigh?"

"Well, as a matter of fact,
these cookies are great,
and thanks for pointing out
I'm a bit overweight."

"I don't mean to offend
and I can sympathize
and show you a way
to drop more than one dress size."

"In order to reduce
you must look to our past
and eat a cave dweller's diet-
one not too vast."

"First, let's focus on
the plant life they would forage.
Each morning I have
hot asparagus porridge."

"With some coffee and sugar
I could choke it down."
"Sorry. There's no coffee,
or sugar, white or brown."

"For lunch I'll have pheasant eggs
and grass-fed goat loins,
which were used for currency
before cash and coins."

"I could handle those
with butter and sour cream."
"Nope. Early man couldn't get dairy
it would seem."

"As evening approaches
I chew some aspen bark.
I harvest it fresh
over at the river park."

"Then I eat sardines
like Paleolithic man."
"That's interesting.
How did they open the can?"

"And about this food,
can I buy it at the store?
Or do I gather it up
off the forest floor?"

"I'd like a slimmer figure,
one that I could brag,
but will body hair grow
and will my knuckles drag?"

"Embrace your primal past
as your resolution!
Lose weight like
the missing link in evolution!"

"Though you say the Paleo diet
has it all,
I'd much rather be fat...
than a Neanderthal!"

January 10, 2015

<u>Strands</u>

"It's been two Saturdays
since Christmas, you know,
and the lights on the house
will all have to go."

This is how my wife
greeted me this morning.
"Please take them down now
to beat the storm warning."

I dressed warmly
and went out to do the job,
determined not
to roll them into a blob.

I plugged them in,
'cause I knew a few were out.
I jiggled the strand
and then started to shout!

Instead of all coming on,
the bulbs went dark.
I shook and screamed,
making the neighbor's dog bark.

I tossed that strand
in a pile on the ground.
I started the next strand
and guess what I found?

Pulling the strand down
I snagged a broken light.
I sliced my hand and shrieked
at the ghastly sight.

I started the next strand
and got to the plug.
It was charcoal black
like a shiny June bug.

I began yanking strands
like I'd gone berserk.
In a few minutes
I was done with my work.

In no time
the entire house was stripped bare.
I stormed inside,
giving my wife quite a scare.

"Oh, no!" my wife said.
"There must be something wrong.
I heard you outside
cursing both bulb and prong."

I went to the fridge
and grabbed out a cold drink.
"Darling, have those lights
driven you to the brink?"

I walked into the room
and popped off the top.
I grinned wide-eyed
and took a gulp of my pop.

She asked of the lights,
"Are they down? Are you through?"
She looked at my wild eyes,
"What did you do?"

I laughed a throaty laugh.
She looked on with fear.
"I threw them out…
I'm buying new ones this year!"

January 17, 2015

<u>Expecting</u>

She gives a smile
in line at the grocery store.
You ask, "How far along are you?"
She smiles no more.

At the hairdresser's you ask
if she's picked out a name.
Then you sit in awkward silence,
silenced by your shame.

During church she's singing.
You notice she has the glow.
She's not glowing when you ask,
"When will you start to show?"

At potluck you ask of
her coming visit from Stork.
She glares at you,
and you walk away without a fork.

Your neighbor likes you.
You ask, "Is it a girl or boy?"
Suddenly you see
to her you're no longer a joy.

The board meets. You ask about
the bun in her oven.
She leaves the conference room
with lots of angry shovin'.

She's joking at a party.
You ask, "You on the nest?"
All of the laughing stops.
She stomps off- and not in jest.

She's leading book club
when you ask of her baby bump.
She slams her book shut.
In your throat you swallow a lump.

You may think of it in terms
of friendly connecting.
But asking if she's pregnant...
what were you expecting!?

January 24, 2015

The Fling

For my whole adult life
I've heard of men who cheat.
I never thought, for another,
my heart could beat.

But the first moment I saw her
my heart took wing,
and I fell victim
in a midafternoon fling.

It was my best friend's girl
and she caught me off guard
by her friendly greeting
as I stepped in the yard.

She had a yellow bow
tied in her golden hair.
Into her almond eyes
I couldn't help but stare.

She led me to the house
with a shake and wiggle.
Hypnotized, I let out
a schoolboy giggle.

Inside the house, my friend said,
"I see that you've met.
I'm running to the store.
I'll be right back, my pet."

Now we were alone
I sat in the La-Z-Boy.
She leapt in my lap—
nothing about her was coy!

She nuzzled up to me
and kissed my neck and face.
I didn't even try
resisting her embrace.

The next thing I knew
we were rolling on the floor,
and didn't stop our game
'til we heard the car door.

I jumped up and tried
to straighten my clothes and hair.
My friend came in—
she threw herself at him right there!

"Easy, Girl!" he smiled.
I knew she wouldn't nark.
He said, "I bet you wish
your girl still had this spark!"

"Speaking of her," I said,
"I should be getting home."
And now I worried,
"Oh, why did I ever roam?"

I checked my shirt for hairs
and started to repent.
I went in, and right away
she caught that girl's scent.

As I made her dinner
her sad eyes said it all.
"After I feed the fish
you and I can play ball."

I filled her dish up,
with senior formula food,
and knew coming clean
is all that would help my mood.

"I must confess," I said,
as I fed the guppy,
"Missi, this afternoon...
I played with a puppy!"

January 31, 2015

Torture

The roof of your mouth
suddenly gets attacked.
Neither tongue nor spoon can ease,
and that's a fact.

You're just standing
when your foot catches fire.
Stomping and scraping
just makes you perspire.

The tag on a new shirt
rubs you the wrong way.
Though useless, you rub back
the entire day.

It's in public
the embarrassing ones dawn.
You twist and lift and shift
but they're never gone.

At midday it strikes
the middle of your back.
And you get no help
from corner, shelf or rack.

Suddenly one arises
deep in your ear.
A key and paperclip
can only get near.

You're never alone
when one invades your nose.
You flick, pinch and pull
but on and on it goes.

Sometimes no matter
how you writhe, squirm or twitch,
you can't get relief from...
a torturous itch!

February 7, 2015
This poem was inspired by everyday items we all use, until we are
told how dangerous they really are!

<u>Daytime Doctor</u>

I was dressing for the gym,
halfway watching a show
with a daytime doctor
telling me what I should know.

He was talking toxics
found in a water bottle.
I snapped to attention
'cause I used the same model!

As he talked BPA's
I knew my bottle was cursed.
I now sat in terror
knowing it had quenched my thirst.

The doctor changed the subject,
he turned to protein shakes,
one filled with hormones,
it was my brand, for goodness sakes!

As he talked injection shots
and pills for dairy cows,
I pondered its consumption
with sweaty, furrowed brows.

The doctor's next topic
was on a flavored sports drink.
Of course, it was my brand,
and by now I couldn't think!

High fructose corn syrup
was his number one concern.
"I drink that!" I cried,
as my stomach started to churn.

Now the doctor lectured
on meal replacement bars.
Again, it was my brand,
and now I was seeing stars!

They were packed full
of genetically modified grain.
"But I eat them all the time!"
I bellowed out in pain.

I watched the show nervously
the entire hour.
Sweating more than at the gym,
I needed a shower.

I looked down at my hands
and I began to panic.
I'd been chewing my nails...
and they're not organic!

February 14, 2015

<u>Desire</u>

I have a man that lives
just over the hill.
Spending time with him
really gives me a thrill.

We have morning coffee
out on the back deck.
My lips dream of warm coffee
and a soft peck.

We lace our shoes
and go for a morning run.
It's as though I'm his shadow
cast by the sun.

He goes to work,
but comes back to me at lunch.
We eat quickly
because he's on a time crunch.

I watch him drive away,
then I take a nap.
I recharge my batteries
and read my map.

I like knowing the terrain
around our place.
I need some hiding spots,
you know, just in case.

He's home for dinner,
but I don't get to cook.
I gaze across his plate
with a longing look.

Nights are hard for me,
I lay there wide awake,
and imagine he breathes
like a dry leaf quake.

But today is Saturday
and that's just fine!
I get to spend it all
with my Valentine!

The weather will be warm
so we'll be outside.
Lounging in the hammock
and on a bike ride.

And wherever he goes
I'll be right there, too.
If only he knew me
and my love so true!

But with my man
I'll cherish being alone.
Yes, it's just me, him...
and my surveillance drone!

February 21, 2015

Arrival

As the days get longer
and the temperatures rise,
signs of an early spring
show up without disguise.

My flowerbed has daffodils
starting to peek.
The crocus and iris
both stick out a green beak.

Two nights ago
a gentle rain washed my stone path.
The earthworms scooted across,
taking their first bath.

Returning geese fly and honk
at the great beyond,
while red-winged black birds
sing beside my backyard pond.

My husband's thick lawn
has an emerging green patch.
He's tinkering in the shed
preparing to thatch.

I too am ready
to start working in the yard,
regardless if winter
deals another card.

As I went to tidy
my garden tool shed,
I saw my first robin
sail past overhead.

I smiled at him
and whistled a happy tune.
Surely he indicated
spring would be here soon.

But a truer sign
than a red breasted glider,
I picked up my gum boots...
and fled from a spider!

February 28, 2015

<u>Morning Attire</u>

After a restless night
without much beauty sleep,
I suggest, from your wife,
a safe distance you keep.

Her morning bed head
is a gnarled, tangled nest,
and for your safety
not mentioning it is best.

Her lips are stuck together
with gross morning breath.
A comment about it
would mean an early death.

Morning stiffness has set in.
She shuffles on past.
A little joke here
would most likely be your last.

Rumpled pajamas
are her morning attire,
and noticing them
would have results quite dire.

Her morning face is frumpy,
drooping and twisted,
and just one smart remark
will have you blacklisted.

"Rise and shine!" you sing.
"I'm glad to see that you're up!"
She pushes on past you
to reach her morning cup.

Though she's groggy,
her movements are habitual.
She pours some coffee,
it's her morning ritual.

Turning, she scowls
and it's not too adorning.
She glares over her mug...
that's her morning warning!

BONUS POEMS

First Story

One hundred and forty-four chicken gizzards. That's gross!
Definitely don't inhale and don't stand too close.

Did you forget your lines at a wedding speech? You're toast!
Just hope you can talk your way out of it with the host.

Did you swallow a magazine down whole? Just digest!
Then don't eat for a while, give your stomach a rest.

I'm so sorry you're ill down a long deep shaft. Get well!
You just might not be sick if down there-you hadn't fell.

You've got some fish on the bottom of your shoe. That's sole!
Where'd you pick it up, down at your secret fishin' hole?

Did you find dirt in your campfire coffee? It's ground!
Now, just cowboy on up, drink it, and don't make a sound.

I learned to read on the school's ground floor. First story!
Helping others love reading? That's a crowning glory.

Breakfast

It's a light golden brown
and it's kinda sticky.
Keeping it off of your chin,
is kinda tricky.

It's really rich and thick
with a nice sweet flavor.
I keep some on my hand
for a snack to savor.

Pour it on your pancakes,
waffles or mashed 'tatoes,
but never, ever waste it,
on stewed tomatoes.

It's good in oatmeal,
if you have grits you'll need it.
Pour lots in your bowl
so you can actually eat it!

One thing I learned is,
keep it out of your hair,
or you'll have to take a bath
and wash everywhere.

So just as sure
as a saddle has a stirrup,
for my breakfast…
I'm having maple syrup!

Pirate

I've wanted to be a pirate
my entire life.
I told my mom,
but she said it would just lead to strife.

"You'd have to cut off a leg
and wear one made out of wood.
You wouldn't be able to run
or play ball very good."

"You'd have to poke out your eye,
and wear a black patch.
You couldn't swing a bat,
and forget playing catch."

"You'd need to chop off your hand
and put on a rusty hook."
You couldn't play football.
You could only stand there and look."

"Then you'd need a smelly parrot
to ride on your shoulder,
and you know you can't have a pet
until you're much older."

"You'd have to live on a ship
that was always on the ocean,
and remember how your stomach is
with all rocking motion?"

"You'd never have to take a bath.
That part wouldn't bother you.
But you'd have plenty of enemies,
and your friends would be few."

"Why have you wanted to be a pirate,
for your entire life?"
"Well, you, see Mom,
I just really, really...want to eat with a knife."

Petals

Pluck its petals,
when you pick a daisy.
It passes a summer day,
that's hot and lazy.

He loves me...
He loves me not...
He loves me...
He loves me not...

Do this over,
'til the petals are gone,
and you'll know the answer,
from the petal you're on.

He loves me...
He loves me not...
He loves me.
That's what I thought!

Guess What

It's got wrinkled, baggy skin,
and a great big middle,
a stiff stubbly chin,
usually covered with spittle.

It has huge tree trunk legs,
and big beefy arms,
very poor hygiene,
and rather short on charms.

It has a loud baritone voice,
along with a shrill whistle.
It's bad-tempered and dangerous,
as a poisonous thistle.

It will chase you up and down,
and make you sweat.
You'll learn lessons in pain,
you won't soon forget.

It's a terrifying beast,
and a cruel creature.
Many names it's been given,
but most call it...Gym teacher!

Printed in the United States
By Bookmasters